Forces and Motion

Sally Hewitt

Chrysalis Education

US publication copyright © 2003 Chrysalis Education. International copyright reserved in all countries. No part of this book may be reproduced in any form without written permission from the publisher.

Distributed in the United States by
Smart Apple Media
1980 Lookout Drive
North Mankato, MN 56003

Copyright © Chrysalis Books PLC 2003

ISBN 1-93233-332-0

The Library of Congress control number 2003102570

Editorial manager: Joyce Bentley
Senior editor: Sarah Nunn
Project editor: Jean Coppendale
Designers: Rachel Hamdi, Holly Mann
Illustrators: Becky Blake, Lisa Smith, and Gwyneth Williamson
Educational consultants: Sally Morgan and Helen Walters

Printed in China

Contents

Words in **bold** are explained in
the Glossary on pages 30–31.

All kinds of forces

Forces are at work everywhere you look, pushing and pulling to make things move. Nothing can move on its own. Without forces, everything would be quite still.

Sliding

Bouncing

Floating

Pulling

Walking

Flying

Swinging

Roller-blading

Spinning

Digging

Pushing

Turning

Cycling

PICTURE SEARCH
★ look at the different ways that things are moving
★ look at things that are still

5

Pushing and pulling

Moving things can go in any direction—backward and forward, up and down, or round and round. The force that moves them either pushes or pulls. This boy is really pushing the ball with the bat.

Opposite forces

When you walk, two **opposite** forces work together. You push down on the ground and the ground pushes up on your foot with the same amount of force. The arrows show the direction of the forces.

downward push

upthrust

Upthrust

The boat is pushing down on the water. It **floats** because the water is pushing it back up with the same amount of force. This force is called **upthrust**.

Wind

Wind is really moving air. Air pushes against the kite and keeps it flying above the ground.

ELASTIC FORCE

Roll some old knee socks into a ball. Then ask an adult to help you tie on a length of sewing **elastic**.

Hold the end of the elastic and bounce the ball.

The force of the ball falling pulls against the elastic and stretches it. The elastic then pulls the ball up as it springs back into shape.

MAGNETISM

Ask an adult to help you stick a strip of magnetic tape onto the bottom of the ball. Scatter some paper clips on the floor. Aim your bouncy ball at the paper clips and try to pick them up. See who can collect the most paper clips in one minute.

Magnets pull objects made of certain kinds of metal towards them with a force called **magnetism**.

START AND STOP

Try pushing and pulling a ball or a toy with wheels to make it move, stop, and change direction.

7

Making work easier

We use all kinds of machines every day to make the work we do easier. Some machines are very simple, such as a pair of scissors or a can opener.

Kitchen scales

Blender

Garlic press

Rolling pin

Nutcrack

Scissors

Peeler

8

PICTURE SEARCH

★ search for all the different jobs that people are doing

★ search for machines that make work easier

Hinge

Iron

Spoon

Pepper grinder

Can opener

9

All kinds of tools

Kitchen **utensils** and **tools** are all simple **machines** that help you to push and pull with more force.

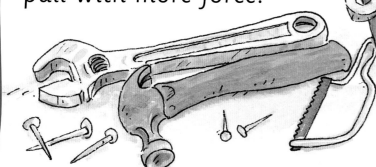

Lever

This spoon is being used as a **lever**. Pushing down on the end of the spoon pushes the lid up.

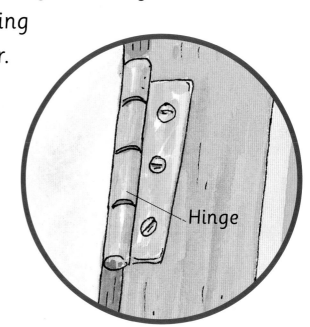

Spoon

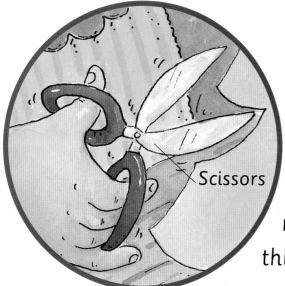

Scissors

Scissors

Scissors are really two levers with handles. They work together to make cutting things easier.

Hinge

A **hinge** is two levers that join two things together, such as a door to a door frame. They make it easier to open and shut doors and lids.

Hinge

JUMPING COIN

Make a lever by **balancing** a ruler on an eraser and putting a coin on one end.

See how high you can make the coin jump by dropping another coin on the other end of the ruler.

SNAP DRAGON

Use a hinge to make a snap dragon.

Place two boxes the same size side by side. Bend a rectangle of strong card in half. Now stick the rectangle across the top, with the fold down the middle of the boxes. Paint on a dragon's face and some teeth. You now have a snap dragon.

LIFT A LOAD

Put a change purse with coins on the end of a ruler. Try and lift it holding the other end.

Now put an eraser under the middle of the ruler for a **pivot**. Put the change purse on one end of the ruler and press down on the other end.

It should be much easier to lift the change purse now.

11

Hard-working machines

In your home, outside in the street, in factories, and on building sites, machines push and pull making the work we have to do much easier.

Pulley

Cement mixer

Wheelbarrow

Tower crane

Truck crane

Digger

Hub

Tire

Forklift truck

Wheel

Gear wheels

Delivery truck

Chain

Pedal

PICTURE SEARCH

★ look for machines with engines
What work are they doing?

★ look for tools without engines
What work are they doing?

Bicycle

13

Getting the work done

Machines and tools help you to do a job. Imagine how long it would take to do this job without a machine.

Forklift truck

Wheels

Wheels are the shape of a circle. They turn round and round on an **axle**. Wheels make it easier to push things along.

Hub   Tire

Wheel

Gears

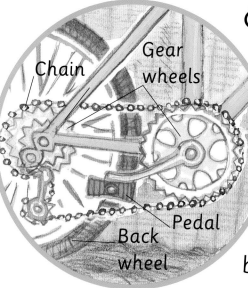

Chain

Gear wheels

Back wheel

Pedal

A bike has two sets of **gear** wheels joined by a chain. When you pedal a bike, one gear wheel turns and this makes the chain move. As the chain moves, it turns the gear wheel joined to the back wheel, and the wheel turns around.

Pulley

A **pulley** is a rope running over a wheel. Pulling down on the rope makes lifting a **load** easier.

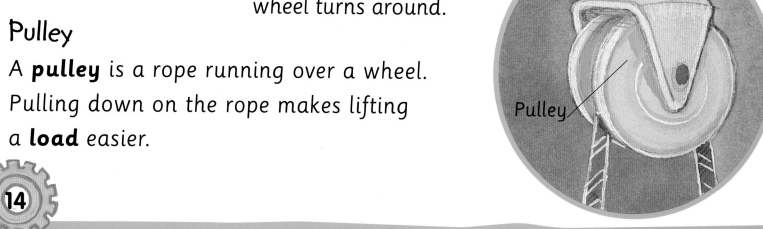

Pulley

MAKE A CART

Wheels have to turn around on a rod called an axle.

1 You need a small box. Cut two drinking straws to make axles wider than the box. Cut out four circles of card for wheels and four rectangles.

2 Punch holes in the middle of the circles and at one end of the rectangles. Stick the rectangles on the box.

3 Push the straws through the holes in the rectangles. Push the wheels on and put modeling clay on the end of the straws to stop the wheels. from falling off. Push your truck to make it move along.

MAKE A PULLEY

Push a knitting needle through a wooden spool to make a pulley wheel. Tie some string to a small bag full of marbles. Run the string around the spool. Pull down on the string. It should be easy to lift the bag with your pulley.

Ask a friend to hold both ends of the knitting needle.

Floating and sinking

An enormous boat floats in the sea but a small pebble **sinks**. Things float or sink in water depending on their shape and size, and what they are made of.

Sailing

Floating

Floatin

Diving

Rowing

Splashi

Swimming

Floating

Sinking

Paddling

PICTURE SEARCH
★ look for things that are floating
★ look for something that is sinking
★ look for things that are moving through the water

17

Shape and size

Things that are heavy for their size, sink in water.
Things that are light for their size, float.

Floating

A beach ball is full of air, which makes it light for its size. It floats because water pushes up on it with the same force as the ball pushes down.

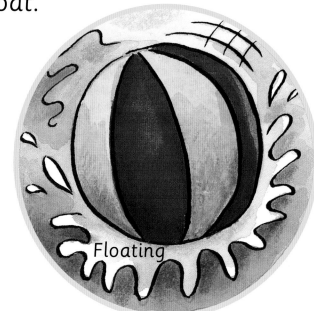

Floating

Boats

Boats made of heavy metal have spaces inside them that are full of air. This makes them light for their size and so they float.

Floating

Sinking

Pebbles are heavy for their size. The water cannot hold them up, so they sink.

Sinking

MAKE A SUBMARINE

Submarines sink when spaces inside them are filled with water. They rise to the **surface** when the spaces are filled with air.

1 Ask an adult to cut three round holes along one side of a small plastic bottle. Pierce three tiny holes along the other side.

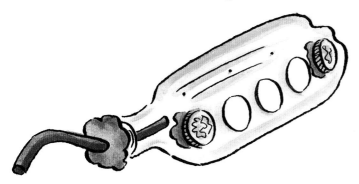

2 Tape two coins at each end of the side with the bigger holes. Fit a plastic tube on the opening and hold it in place with modeling clay.

3 Fill the bottle with water to make it sink in the bath. Blow through the tube to fill it with air to make it rise.

FEEL UPTHRUST

Push down on an air-filled ball in a bowl of water. Feel the water pushing back up on the ball. You won't be able to sink it. Let it go and it will jump out of the water!

SINK A BOAT

Make a boat shape out of modeling clay or kitchen foil and float it in a bowl of water. How many marbles can you fill it with before it sinks?

Friction

When two surfaces rub together, they make a force called **friction**. Smooth surfaces rubbing together make less friction than rough surfaces.

Toboggan

Sliding

Ice skates

Snow boots

Ski lift

Snow-
mobile

Snow
board

Skis

Snowplow

Rubbing

PICTURE SEARCH
look for rough surfaces
look for smooth surfaces

Snow boots

Gripping

21

Slowing down

A book won't keep on moving when you give it a push. The book rubs against the table and makes friction. Friction slows the book down and stops it.

Smooth surfaces

Ice skates and ice both have smooth surfaces. Ice skates slide easily over ice because they make very little friction.

Sliding

Gripping

Rough surfaces

The sole of a snow boot has a rough surface. It makes friction as it rubs against the snow and stops you from slipping.

Heat

When you have cold hands, rub them together. Friction makes heat, so rubbing your hands together warms them up.

Rubbing

RASP AND RUB

Use friction to make a **percussion** instrument. Stick rectangles of rough sandpaper onto two empty boxes the same size. Rub the sides with the sandpaper together in time to music. They make an amazing rasping sound!

MAKE A SLIDE

Try sliding an eraser, a coin, a jar lid, a wooden block, and a small cardboard box around on a metal tray. How well do they move? Now wipe a thin layer of cooking oil over the tray and slide the objects again.

Oil makes the friction less, so now they slide around easily.

MAKE FOOTPRINTS

Sprinkle talcum powder onto a sheet of black paper. Now press the soles of different shoes into the powder to make footprints. Look at the prints. Which soles will be best for walking on slippery surfaces?

Moving through air

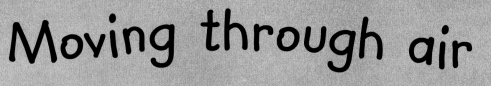

Airplanes have a good shape for flying and powerful engines to push them through the air. Parachutes are shaped for floating slowly downwards.

Helicopter

Hot-air balloon

Glider

Nose

Biplane

Passenger plane

Wing

Jet planes

PICTURE SEARCH
★ look for things that can fly and float in the air
★ look for things that can't fly

Propeller plane

Propeller

Hang glider

Parachute

Kite

Windsock

25

Floating and flying

Air collects under a parachute and pushes up against it as it falls. This slows the parachute down and lets it float to the ground to give the parachutist a safe landing.

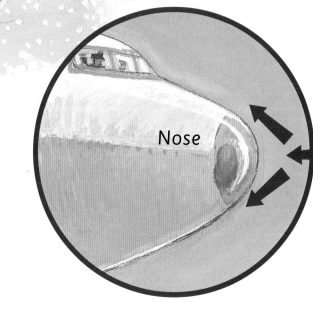

Nose

Movi
air

Streamline shapes

Airplanes have smooth, **streamlined** shapes so that air can slip over them easily.

Moving air

Wings

The way air moves over an airplane's wings creates a force that lifts it into the air.

Propellers

Propellers spin round and round creating a force that pushes the plane along.

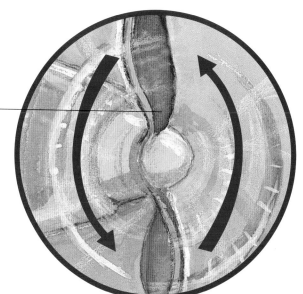

Spinning propeller

MAKE A PARACHUTE

Tape four lengths of string around the edge of a big paper plate. Tie the strings to a small toy. Throw the parachute up in the air and watch it float slowly down to the ground.

FALLING PAPER

Drop a sheet of paper and watch it float to the ground. Air pushes against it and holds it up. Now crumple the paper and drop it. It falls much more quickly *because the paper takes up less space, so there is less paper for the air to push against.*

MAKE PAPER DARTS

Try folding paper darts in different shapes.

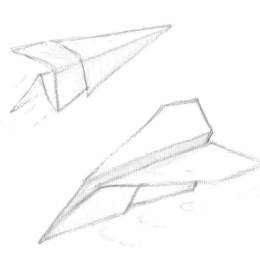

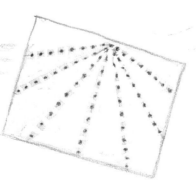

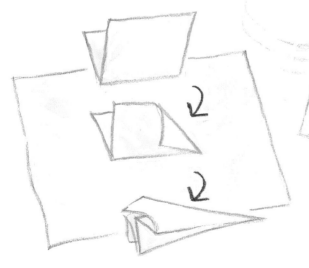

Which are the *best* shapes for flying through the air? Which one flies the furthest?

More things to learn about forces

Gravity

Sir Isaac Newton discovered the force of gravity after watching an apple fall from a tree. Gravity pulls everything down toward the center of Earth.

Surface tension

Surface tension is a force that makes water look as though it has a stretchy skin. An insect such as a water strider is small and light enough to walk on the skin without breaking it.

Balance

You don't fall over when you ride a bike because of balance. Everything balances evenly around a point called the center of gravity. Too much weight on one side could make you lose your balance and fall over.

Center of gravity

Centrifugal force

Centrifugal force is at work on this fairground ride. As the ride spins around, centrifugal force pushes the children in their chairs away from the pole in the center.

BE A SCIENTIST

★ Keep your eyes open and watch how and why things move.

   Notice things changing—shadows changing length, ice melting.

★ Ask questions about what you see—Why? How? What if?

★ Try things out for yourself—but see warnings below.

Be careful

★ Don't try any experiments without asking an adult first.

★ Don't use sharp or hot things or make mixtures by yourself.

putty

rubber bands

useful things box

marbles

You need:

★ A box of things for your experiments: plastic bottles, cardboard tubes, poster putty, sticky tape, ruler, scissors, magnetic strip.

★ Add to your box as you go along.

Glossary

Axle

A rod that goes through the middle of a wheel. Wheels turn round on an axle.

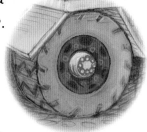

Balance

When something is balanced, it means that its weight is spread evenly. If you were carrying a heavy bag in one hand and nothing in the other, you would be unbalanced.

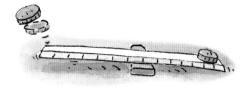

Elastic

Elastic is a kind of material that stretches when you pull it and springs back into shape when you let it go.

Float

To float means to stay on the surface of water. An object floats when water pushes up on it with

enough force to hold it up in the water.

Forces

Forces push and pull on things to make them move, speed up, slow down, or change shape.

Friction

Friction is a kind of force that happens when two things rub together.

Gears

Gear are a set of wheels with teeth. When one gear wheel turns, its teeth turn the wheel next to it.

Hinge

A hinge joins two things together, such as a door to a frame or a lid to a box. It lets the door and the lid open and close.

Lever

A lever is a bar that makes lifting things easier. When you push down on one end of a lever, the other end can lift something up with more force.

Load

A load is something that is carried. A bag of shopping and a bucket of cement are both kinds of a load.

Machine

We use machines to make work easier. A crane is a machine that lifts heavy loads and an iron presses creases out of clothes.

Magnetism

Magnetism is a kind of force. A magnet uses the force of magnetism to pull objects made of iron towards it.

Opposite

Things that are opposite are quite different from each other. Up is the opposite of down, and a push is the opposite of a pull.

Percussion

You make a sound on a percussion instrument by hitting or shaking it. A drum and maracas are both percussion instruments.

Pivot

A pivot is the point on which something turns. A seesaw balances and goes up and down on a pivot.

Pulley

A wheel with a rope running around it. Pulling down on one end of the rope helps make lifting a load on the other end easier.

Sink

To sink means to fall to the bottom of water. An object sinks when it pushes down on water with more force than the water is pushing it up.

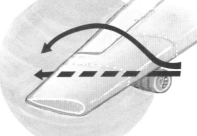

Streamlined

Air and water move easily over a streamlined shape. Airplanes and speed boats have streamlined shapes for traveling through air and water.

Submarine

A submarine is a kind of boat that can move along under water as well as on the surface.

Surface

The surface is the outside, the top, or the skin of something.

Tools

Tools are simple machines that help us to do a job. A hammer is a tool for pushing in nails. Scissors are tools for cutting.

Upthrust

Water pushes up against objects with a force called upthrust.

Utensil

A utensil is another word for tool. Knives and forks, rolling pins, and whisks are utensils we use in the kitchen for cooking and eating.

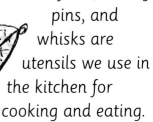

Index